T0194761

KEY ELEMENTS OF STRESS, EXHAUSTION, AND BURNOUT— BUT I'M REJUVENATED!

A GUIDE FOR INDIVIDUALS AND ORGANIZATIONS

Dr. Darlynne Kerr

authorHOUSE

AuthorHouse™
1663 Liberty Drive
Bloomington, IN 47403
www.authorhouse.com
Phone: 833-262-8899

Published by AuthorHouse 02/21/2022

ISBN: 978-1-6655-5224-0 (sc)
ISBN: 978-1-6655-5223-3 (hc)
ISBN: 978-1-6655-5225-7 (e)

Library of Congress Control Number: 2022903161

Print information available on the last page.

Design Credit to: Lenoy McBride

This book is printed on acid-free paper.

CONTENTS

DEDICATION

A special dedication, first and foremost, to my mother, the late Hazel Kerr: You have made me who I am today—without you I would not have made it. You have instilled in me the core essence of love, determination, and resilience. We have had many special moments. I will always remember them and your warmth and giving spirit, and I am blessed to have you as my mom. To my grandmother, the late Hattie Josephs: You have instilled in me what a virtuous women is and to hold on to God's unchanging Hand. To my cousin, the late Albertha Wilkinson: You have departed a tremendous amount of wisdom in my life, which I carry with me today. I thank you for stepping in as a mother figure when my mother was absent. I miss you all tremendously and wish you were here to share this moment with me. I love you very much!

To the heaven-sent individuals who stepped in as a mother figure in my life—the late Shirley Davidson, Mrs. Ellison, the late Mrs. Valery Nobel, Dora Little John, and the late Mrs. Vaughn and late Mrs. Mack—You have interceded for me, encouraged me, instilled knowledge and wisdom in me. I love you!

I want to give a special dedication to my farther, Herman Kerr. Dad, you have been very patient with me and have instilled in me a lot of wisdom and I am very grateful for you. This journey of completion would not have been possible without you. I know you only want the best for me, so I hope that I have made you proud of me. Words cannot describe how much I love you!

I dedicate this book to my family and extended family: Hermen Kerr, Dwayne Kerr, Arthur Joseph, Antoinette Palmer, Paulette Tucker, Lisa Easn, Teresa Oliver, Zatone Frazier, Miguel Centron, and the late Jose Centron. Words cannot describe what you guys mean to me. I'm thankful that God brought you all into my life. Through the ups and downs, we have all been there for each other. Your tenacity to achieve no matter what others think of you or say speaks multitudes in my life. The talks, shelter, advice, guidance, and love will carry me throughout my life. Thank you for sharing your lives with me. Love you always! Thank you for supporting me through this journey and believing in me. I hope I have made you proud. We all have experienced different parts of this journey together, so thank you for helping me to see the light, for having my back, for encouraging me, for praying for me, and for supporting me through it all. I hope that I have shown that we can overcome anything as long as we have each other and hold on to God. I hope I have shown we should never give up on our dreams and we can determine what our futures will be. We are a family and there is nothing stronger than the love of God within a family. When times get tough, remember to "Never Give Up" on your dreams, goals, aspirations, or destiny. I love you all to pieces! You all are the corner stone of me.

ACKNOWLEDGMENTS

To My Spiritual Father

Giving honor to God, my Lord Jesus Christ, you are my friend. Confidante, thank you for saving my life, for anointing my soul, and for giving me the strength, endurance, insight, grace, mercy, and heavy favor to excel beyond my dreams to inspire others.

To My Family

Thank you for being there and guiding me through life. Thank you for taking the time to give me guidance and advice and showing me the path to life, regardless of how hard it gets, is to overcome the hurdles and never give up. You inspired me to work harder than I had before by setting an outstanding example in life. You have made me think bigger and go after what is important. When times were rough, you came through. I could not have done this without you. I am truly thankful you are a part of my life.

To My Spiritual Family

To Bishop Eddie Long, thank you for filling in as my spiritual father. Thank you for inspiring me to set high expectations and to do my best at all times. To Pastor Simeon Moultrie, Nikki Moultrie, and Pastor Greg, thank you for imparting the knowledge of God and prayer in my life when times were tough during my relocation.

To My Extended Family and Friends

I owe many thanks to my friends, who hold a special place in my heart: Valencia Sales, Alesha Vanager, Tony Scott, Alex Braggs, Cynthia Perez, Salleya Reese, Demetria Coleman, Krystal Coleman, Shariees Blackwood, Joseph Pope, Mary Miller-Wall, Tamelva Brown, Dr. Shaunte Davidson-Baggling,

Michelle, Carolyn Hail, Courtney Randolph, Deboris Gallant, the Lovell family, Ricardo Williams, Joi Nichols, the late ITury Mack, the Ellison family, Mickey McBride, Astrid Milo, Donald Harper, James Saunders, Keith Hewlett, Lyte, Wanda Patterson, Craig, Carlos, Fritz, the late C.J., Dylan, Sincere, Stacy, Bruizer, R.R., Khaotic Kings, my entrepreneur partners, and everyone's families. If I have forgotten anyone, please forgive me. There are so many that have impacted my life. You are all special to me. We have all shared special moments throughout this journey together. Thank you all for your support.

To all of my cousins, nephews, nieces, aunts and uncles, you have shown so much support through my journey.

To Dr. John Eze, Dr. Keisha Malcolm, Dr. Regina DeLay, Dr. Cheryl Gleen-Snooks, Dr. Charlene Gail, Dr. Duane Gordon, Dr. Darlene Harris, and Dr. Jeffery Ryans. When times were rough you guys came through. I am truly thankful for all of you being a part of my life.

To My Colleagues:

To Matthew Lassiter's, Jessica Henderson's office and colleagues, thank you truly for putting in your time, knowledge, and pushing me to the highest level possible I could go. In addition, I appreciate you for showing me what a true leader is and taking control of your dreams, passions, your life, and accomplishing your goals. I will always be grateful; it has allowed me to grow in all areas and has given me a different perspective on life. To Dr. Mitchell's office, thank you for giving me the opportunity to be a part of your organization, family, and instilling many key attributes. It helped me grow, I will always be grateful.

You all hold a special place in my heart. I am thankful to have you in my life. You have challenged me and inspired me in every way possible. Thank you for showing me how important it is to take control of your dreams and your life, and to accomplish your goals. You have made me think outside the box and inspired me to change my perspective. We have all shared special moments throughout this journey together. Thank you all for your support. I will always be grateful.

PREFACE

This story takes you through a journey I experienced in the workplace arena more often than not. I worked in a healthcare facility for approximately 15 years in different spectrums of this industry and ventured into other industries that face the same issues. In this career setting, I witnessed the phenomenon that many workers start to become extremely exhausted and, as time progresses, become distant from other staff and withdraw from social interactions. They appear overwhelmed with work responsibilities, due to others calling in sick or arriving late (and/or they call in sick or arrive late themselves). As my career advanced and I worked in other healthcare sectors, I saw many employees quit because of lack of resources, lack of support, and the prolonged stress level. Many employees have been impacted by the amount of duties they have and not knowing what is going on or how to handle it. Furthermore, I experienced similar symptoms, feeling extremely tired and drained to the point that I was physically getting sick six to seven times a year. I was so overwhelmed I could not focus on what I needed to do, which also impacted my memory process.

These symptoms led me to question what was going on, why, and how things could change. I began to inquire about the amount of stress I was under—like many others—and the root causes of this stress. This is when I recognized that individuals who share these symptoms of extreme fatigue, disconnection, and questioning oneself are experiencing *burnout*. Burnout is a major phenomenon nationwide and has been the cause of many tragic situations, including depression, anxiety, and even suicide and workplace violence. I chose to focus my dissertation study on burnout in the private practice setting, to tell the story of burnout so that individuals and organizations can understand its causes, impacts, and how to deal with it.

Through this book, I aim to inform individuals and management about the ways that burnout can impact individuals and/or the workplace. Burnout can be decreased greatly if different interventions are implemented to reduce prolonged stress. This book provides background on the causes of burnout, the different reasons burnout happens, and the various symptoms people experienced when burned out. As I researched this phenomenon, I wanted to provide ideas for individuals and management to enhance their workplace to reduce and, hopefully, eliminate burnout. Ultimately, this book will educate readers and provide an understanding of burnout. This information and strategies in this book will help individuals enhance their life and that of those around them.

INTRODUCTION

France Telecom, a well-known telecommunications company, was an established provider of Internet, mobile, and TV services in France with, until 2008, a record of success. However, from 2008–2009, 35 of the company's employees committed suicide, the tragic product of years of frustration and a culture of bullying within the workplace. The company's CEO, Didier Lombard, along with two executives resigned in 2010 as a result, and the company faced an uncertain future (Venturi, 2014). This case highlights the extreme and negative outcomes stress and burnout can have for both individuals and the organizations in which they work—outcomes that span multiple fields, locations, and types of workplaces.

Within the United States, more than 40% of full- and part-time workers have reported high and increasing levels of job stress, and 25% reported that their job was the main source of stress in their lives (Weaver, 2003). This stress can have wide-ranging physical, social, psychological, and economic implications. There are many sources of stress within the workplace, ranging from heavy workloads, to unclear demands/expectations, to working with limited resources, to uncontrollable situations, to interpersonal conflict and bullying (Hazell, 2010; Jamal, 2010). Chronic stress develops when an individual does not recover from the prior workday, leading to feelings of being overwhelmed and burned out.

Indeed, one of the highest risks of stress in the workplace is that it can lead to *burnout*, a state of extreme emotional depletion, fatigue, and loss of motivation that impacts individuals' job performance, productivity, and success. Indeed, employee stress and burnout has become an alarming issue within the United States. One study, for example, found 63% of employees did not feel in control of their emotions; 39% felt high levels of stress due to work responsibilities; 53% needed to take repetitive breaks; and 46% experienced absences from stress and personal interactions (Jayson, 2012). Burnout also leads workers to develop negative attitudes towards their work and others, leading to loss of focus, work dissatisfaction, increased absences, intent to leave, high turnover, and lack of commitment to the organization (Potter et al., 2010).

While burnout affects all occupations, workers in service roles (i.e., those that care for others) experience higher levels of burnout (Maslach, Schaufeli, & Leiter, 2001). For example, healthcare workers may become attached to patients and emotionally impacted by their patients' outcomes. This can lead to a related condition called *compassion fatigue*, where workers lose their ability to connect and empathize with others. For example, one study of oncology staff found that the level of care provided to patients took a toll on the staff, creating large amounts of stress in the workplace, psychological exhaustion, and employee dissatisfaction (Potter et al., 2010).

Stress and burnout in the workplace present a pressing issue that leadership must address to ensure the health of their employees and the organization as a whole. To combat stress and burnout, both leadership and individuals need to recognize first their signs and symptoms, and then focus on decreasing stressors and creating a healthy workplace and supportive environment. In this book, I provide a guide to help both individual employees and organizational leadership identify, manage, and prevent stress and burnout in the workplace. In doing so, I provide an evidence-based approach centered on my doctoral research findings (Kerr, 2017), as I describe below.

An Evidenced-Based Approach

This book stems from the research I conducted during my doctoral work and the findings of that research, along with the body of scholarly literature I reviewed during the research process. In my qualitative, exploratory study, I examined the factors that triggered burnout among six full-time administrative employees in private practice settings in South Carolina. Overall, I explored the lived experience of the workers to identify the challenges they faced with stress and burnout in their workplace.

To gather data, I first administered to participants a 15-question demographic questionnaire that identified their age, gender, income, work status, work position, job title, work experience, occupation, signs of burnout experienced, work setting, staff size, and marital status. I then conducted semistructured interviews with the participants (45–60 minutes in length), which asked a series of open-ended questions about their experience with stress and burnout. After transcribing the interviews, I analyzed the data via the software program NVivo to identify themes that informed the findings. While these findings were based on a small sample of administrative staff working in medical and legal fields, their experiences with burnout may be relevant to other workers who face similar issues. Below, I describe the participants in more detail so we can get to know the voices that informed this work.

The Voices

The findings of my study were based on the experiences of six administrative staff working full-time in private medical or legal practices in South Carolina. All participants were Caucasian or African American females ranging in age from 31 to 50.[1] Some women had children, while others did not; similarly, some were married, while some were single. The women had diverse hobbies including cooking, sports, music, surfing, and travel. In their professional lives, as administrators, they had a wide range of duties including (but not limited to): communication (e.g., interacting with clients, communicating with the courts, phone/email duties); finances (e.g., managing client payments, bill payments); scheduling (e.g., managing the calendar, rescheduling, managing reminders and set-ups); other paperwork (e.g., filing, drafting meetings and letters for the company, typing dictation, drafting); marketing; and

---

[1] Originally, the study was open to men and women from all racial/ethnic backgrounds in North and South Carolina. However, only Caucasian and African American women in South Carolina chose to participate in the study.

handling various types of legal claims. Most importantly, all participants felt stressed, overwhelmed, exhausted, and/or emotionally depressed in their work environment—feelings that drew them to participate in the study.

In This Book

Stress and burnout negatively impact both workers and their workplaces in a myriad of ways, ranging from worker dissatisfaction, to emotional and psychological issues, to exhaustion and fatigue, to high turnover, decreased productivity, and decreased job performance. As such, it is essential for organizational leaders to intervene and develop a system that will reduce the stress levels of their employees (Michie, 2002). In this book, I provide a guide to stress and burnout in the workplace for both individual employees and organizational leadership. Stemming from my study of burnout among administrative staff in private practice in South Carolina, in this book I highlight the signs, symptoms, and effects of burnout so that workers and managers can understand, address, and hopefully prevent stress and burnout in the workplace.

More specifically, in Chapter 1, "Understanding Stress and Burnout," I review the concepts of stress, burnout, and compassion fatigue, examining their causes and how they can be measured in the workplace.

In Chapter 2, "The Impact of Stress and Burnout in the Workplace," I look at how stress and burnout affects employees physical health, workplace behaviors, and job performance, and their effects on an organization's success.

Then, in Chapter 3, "Recognizing Stress and Burnout," I move to a more practical discussion of the signs and symptoms of stress and burnout, and the role of coping mechanisms in employees' ability to manage stress and burnout.

In Chapter 4, "Creating a Healthy Workplace," I continue this discussion to look at how both individuals and organizations can prevent stress and burnout by increasing workplace activities and the role of management in such efforts.

In Chapter 5, "Becoming Rejuvenated Again," I provide tips for individuals and organizations to help decrease stress and health from burnout.

Finally, in "Closing Remarks," I offer a summary of the key themes of the book and brief recommendations for individuals, organizations, and scholars looking to combat stress and burnout in the workplace.

CHAPTER 1

UNDERSTANDING STRESS AND BURNOUT

Stress and burnout are major problems nationwide and, indeed, globally in all sectors of the workforce (Hazell, 2010). Understanding stress and burnout is the first step in tackling this problem both as individuals and in the workplace. It is important to highlight here that stress and burnout, when experienced by individuals, affect every aspect of their personal and professional lives. So, what happens in the workplace not only affects workers' performance and success in their jobs, it also impacts their ability to function and succeed in their home lives and personal relationships with others (spouse, friends, families, etc.), as well as their overall health and well-being (physical, mental, emotional, spiritual, economic, etc.). Therefore, stress and burnout are holistic problems that have wide-ranging and significant impacts both inside and outside the workplace. In this chapter, I explain the concepts of job stress, burnout, and compassion fatigue, and discuss their causes within the workplace.

What is Stress?

There are many definitions of *stress*. Stress is a serious condition, which can cause an individual to become physically and psychologically ill. Stress encompasses physical and emotional traits, and some of these traits are directly proportionate to strain within the workplace. Stress can display itself in an acute or behavioral matter. Some acute responses include anxiety, depression, and fatigue, whereas behavioral responses include being withdrawn or aggressive (Michie, 2002). The most common response to emotional stress is anxiety and frustration (Nixon, Mazzola, Bauer, Krueger, & Spector, 2011).

Job stress is when a person feels uptight, apprehensive, and is suffering from work responsibilities. Job stress is a combination of an employee's mentality and feelings of inconvenience from the job (Lambert, Hogan, Cheeseman, & Barton-Bellessa, 2013). Job stress is one potential reaction to the atmosphere of or a situation in the workplace, which impacts the individual's psychological and physical state. Job stress results when individuals do not know how to handle particular circumstances in the workplace, such as tasks that are overwhelming (Jamal, 2010; Michie, 2002). Stress may also occur when an individual is straining in their workplace environment, resources are not sufficient, or they are not able to manage or cope with the demands of the job. How individuals handle stress is a major part of their professional identity and work conduct (Maslach et al., 2001).

Chronic stress occurs when the worker is not given time to recover from the prior workday, and experiences prolonged stress over time. This can lead to feelings of being overwhelmed and burned out. The longer the stress continues, the more severe the impacts can have on both the worker and organization.

What is Burnout?

Burnout is a term originally coined by Freudenberger (1974). Freudenberger conducted a seminal study of volunteers in the human service field who worked at clinics, support homes, hot lines, and other therapeutic communities. These workers faced challenging situations and had constant interaction with people. Freudenberger wanted to understand the demands placed upon these workers and how the demands impacted their psychological and physical health. Freudenberger (1974) found that burnout occurs when an individual exhausts their energy level by completing excessive amounts of requests. By looking at how their emotional states changed over time because of this phenomenon, Freudenberger came to an understanding of burnout as characterized by emotional depletion and loss of motivation and commitment. Freudenberger also agreed with the dictionary definition of burnout, which is "to fail, wear out, or become exhausted by making excessive demands on energy."

Upon further research, Maslach and Jackson (1981) expanded this definition of burnout to displaying the three symptoms of emotional exhaustion, lack of identity (depersonalization), and decrease in personal or self-accomplishment (inefficacy). Burnout has subsequently been referred to as a syndrome, which consists of feeling extremely overwhelmed, exhausted, and disconnected from others.

Pines and Aronson (1983) defined burnout as a state of physical, emotional, and mental exhaustion that "typically occurs as a result of working with people over long periods of time in situations that are emotionally demanding" (as cited in Pines, 1993, p. 263). Broadening the definition to all fields, Schaufeli and Greenglass (2001) defined burnout as a state of physical, emotional, and mental exhaustion that results from long-term involvement in work situations that are emotionally demanding (as cited in Engelbrecht, 2005, p. 33).

While burnout can happen to anyone, it most affects service occupations, where workers care for others and/or have a constant interaction with people (Jamal, 2010; Maslach et al., 2001). This includes, for example, police, counselors, teachers, nurses, social workers, psychiatrists, psychologists, attorneys, physicians, and administrators (Maslach & Pines, 1978). Service occupations are most affected because of the interpersonal relationships that such work requires.

Many service workers in institutional settings are usually committed to the cause, give of themselves, work extended hours, and do not get compensated well for their efforts (Freudenberger, 1974). For example, medical professionals may become emotionally attached to patients with whom they work on a daily basis. To take care of others requires workers to give of themselves empathetically—to *care*. This can have a large emotional toll, especially when patients experience hardship and suffering. It can also lead to emotional exhaustion.

Emotional exhaustion occurs when an individual becomes overwhelmed with the emotional demands placed upon them by others in the workplace, which exhausts their emotionally abilities (Maslach, 2003; Maslach & Jackson, 1981). They may feel they have used all their resources and cannot give any more (Lee, Lovell, & Brotheridge, 2010). Emotional exhaustion causes an individual to not have an acceptable amount of vitality to prepare for the coming work day, no way to reload for the next day, and not being able to supply further services to others (Maslach & Jackson, 1981). Emotional exhaustion leads to *depersonalization*, when an employee starts to have negative emotions toward others and detaches from the situation. As a consequence of this emotional strain, especially when it occurs over a long period of time, this turns into *compassion fatigue.*

Compassion Fatigue

In this book, I view compassion fatigue as a component of burnout, which is intrinsically implied whenever the term *burnout* is used. When workers experience compassion fatigue, they lose their ability to care, to connect, and empathize with others. They may feel numb to the situations and people around them, become distanced, and withdraw from social interactions. They may start to separate themselves from the people they interact with in the workplace to avoid the level of stress they encounter (Maslach, 2003).

This may ultimately lead workers to exhibit "detached, callous and even dehumanized responses" (Maslach, 2003, p. 5), and to become detached from concerns about clients/patients' needs, affecting the workers' ability to work with and for others. This is ultimately a sign of psychological exhaustion, which often leads to physical exhaustion and employee dissatisfaction. The longer a worker is in a given role, the higher the risk of compassion fatigue.

Ultimately, stress, burnout, and compassion fatigue prevent workers from being able to do their jobs effectively and successfully. Employees may express that they no longer want to come to work because they suffer from extreme fatigue, separation from people, and mental and physical illness issues caused by burnout (Potter et al., 2010). Burnout, in turn, leads workers to incur negative feelings about themselves and their sense of worth, as they cannot succeed in their jobs and lives and may feel guilt for how they are treating others and conducting themselves in the workplace.

Furthermore, the negative emotions these workers experience may develop into feelings of reduced personal accomplishment (Maslach, 2003; Maslach & Jackson, 1981). Workers may become unsatisfied with themselves and discontent with their work achievements. As a result, they may display a bad attitude toward their work performance and toward their clients/patients (Maslach, 2003; Maslach & Jackson, 1981). The worker, as a result, may become cynical. Cynicism further leads to reduced personal accomplishment toward self and other matters (Lee et al., 2010; Maslach & Leiter, 2005). Consequently, without the right tools to cope with these emotions, workers may look to find alternative situations that relieve their stress (which may be unhealthy, such as turning to alcohol/substance abuse), or feel they need to leave the workplace entirely.

Causes of Stress and Burnout

Burnout presents itself in workers when they are not exposed to a positive atmosphere. There are several job-related stressors that prevent workers from being successful. Indeed, burnout results from being chronically stressed due to prolonged job stressors that result from facing challenging situations. These challenges can range from situations arising from the nature of the work itself, to interpersonal factors, to heavy or unrealistic work demands/expectations, to organizational factors. These include (but are not limited to):

- Heavy workloads/responsibilities,
- Unclear demands/expectations,
- Role ambiguity or role conflict,
- Lack of resources,
- Long work hours,

- Organizational constraints,

- Lack of control,

- Unpredictability/instability/ambiguity in the workplace,

- Bullying and interpersonal conflict,

- Lack of opportunities for professional development,

- Lack of social support,

- Management style,

- Organizational structure,

- Organizational demographics, and

- Environment of the location.

The worker's coping mechanisms, mental health status, and ability to manage stress also impact their likelihood to experience burnout, and thus there are individual factors that play a role as well.

Measuring Burnout

How do we know, however, that burnout really occurs? Beyond anecdotal evidence, within the scholarly literature, researchers have developed tools to measure burnout among individuals within organizations. The most notable and widely used of these tools—used in over 90% of burnout research—is the Maslach Burnout Inventory (MBI) (Maslach & Jackson, 1981), which I also utilized in my doctoral study. The MBI is a quantitative survey that measures three specific areas, in keeping with the definition of burnout: emotional exhaustion (EE), depersonalization (DP), and reduced personal accomplishment (PA). The tool measures 22 areas with various subitems that accommodate these three essential elements. The results are displayed with three different scores, one for each essential area, identifying the score as high or low. The high and low scores indicate the level of burnout; when there are high scores of EE and DP and a low score of PA, this indicates a severe amount of burnout (Galanakis, Moraitou, Garivalkis, & Stalikas, 2009). The MBI has been used both within the United States and internationally, and has been translated into different languages and altered into various versions to accommodate different occupations.

Summary

Stress and burnout are major concerns nationwide and globally in all occupations. Stress and burnout result when workers cannot cope with the ongoing demands, challenges, and environment of the workplace. Stress and burnout have a range of symptoms and outcomes, affecting workers holistically in every aspect of their lives. These concepts are intrinsically linked, and impact workers' ability to perform their duties efficiently and successfully. In the next chapter, I explain further the impacts of stress and burnout in the workplace, specifically looking at job performance and organizational success.

CHAPTER 2

THE IMPACTS OF STRESS AND BURNOUT IN THE WORKPLACE

Now that we understand what stress and burnout are, in this chapter, I explain how stress and burnout affect individuals and the workplace. I begin this discussion by looking at how stress and burnout affect individuals' physical health and, thus, the time they spend at work, before moving to examine the workplace, and specifically, workplace behaviors, job performance, and organizational success.

Worker Health

Sohail and Rehman (2015) stated, "stress at work leads to physical and mental hazards. At an extreme, long-term stress at work creates psychological disorders which results in the absence of employees from the job" (p. 112). While stress and burnout are often seen as psychological issues, they have wide-ranging physical and psychological health effects that lead workers to have increased lateness and absences due to being sick or unfit for work.

Physical symptoms include trouble sleeping, exhaustion and fatigue, along with headaches, colds, back ache and other musculoskeletal pain, eyestrain, dizziness, appetite and stomach problems, restlessness, and trouble breathing (Freudenberger, 1975; Nixon et al., 2011). Often, workers may ignore the physical symptoms, thinking it will go away. As time goes on, however, the workers become more ill with more persistent physical symptoms, which end up requiring treatment and, thus, time off work (Ekstedt & Fagerberg, 2005).

Psychological effects may impact the employee's ability to work and function effectively in interpersonal relationships. Psychological impacts include anxiety, depression and other mental health issues, which may in extreme cases lead to suicide. Other impacts include issues with self-esteem and self-confidence, mood swings, issues with confusion or memory, or other mental issues,

Worker health has large implications for the organization, as both absences from work and insurance/compensation can often be costly to the organization. Moreover, if the worker is not able to fulfill their duties and takes prolonged periods of time off work or leaves the workplace entirely, in addition to loss of productivity, the organization must incur the costs of loss of knowledge and rehiring, both of which are detrimental to the organization.

Workplace Behaviors

Burnout can have a major impact on other workers in the company and manifest itself in different manners (Maslach et al., 2001). When experiencing stress and burnout, workers may lose focus, adopt a negative attitude, and experience dissatisfaction in the workplace (Potter et al., 2010). When an individual is not able to think clearly, they can make an irrational decision, which may affect their job and the company. It can also lead them to become irritable and angry or to withdraw from social interactions with others.

Burnout is affiliated with negative workplace behaviors, which include enhanced absences, resignation, alcohol abuse and smoking, continuous job changes, decreased quality of service, increased coffee consumption, as well as social and economic problems (Galanakis et al., 2009). These behaviors also extend to how workers interact with others, including staff and clients/patients, which impacts the quality of their work and services provided.

Job Performance

Burnout causes workers to not perform effectively in their occupations due to the effects of the associated symptoms. The signs of burnout can be severe and cause workers to disconnect themselves from others, which in the end can have negative effects on staff performance (Maslach, 2003).

Stress and burnout thus impact the level and quality of service workers provide to clients/customers/patients. Maslach et al. (2001) stated that when an employee decides to continue at an organization that does not fulfill them, their productivity will decline and their loyalty is not the same. Due to the physical and psychological symptoms that accompany stress and burnout, it affects workers':

- Productivity,
- Efficiency and effectiveness,
- Quality of work/services provided,
- Interpersonal relationships,
- Job success,
- Motivation,
- Morale,
- Loyalty to the organization,
- Organizational commitment, and
- Retention.

All of these factors, in turn, affect the long-term success of the organization.

Organizational Success

Stress and burnout have substantial practical and economic implications and costs for organizations, as well as the long-term sustainability and success of the organization as a whole. Workers who experience high levels of stress are often unsatisfied with their jobs, which cause the organization to have a higher level of turnover (Zhang, Tsingan, & Zhang, 2013). Indeed, burnout can lead to increased intent to leave, early retirement, turnover, and attrition, causing workers to change or leave their roles/jobs. Turnover is a major issue that affects "employees' morale, team performance and productivity" (Green, Miller, & Aarons, 2013, p. 374). High turnover can interrupt the quality of care given and existing relationships. Turnover thus incurs large costs for employers due to the costs of rehiring/retraining as well as quality of services rendered.

This trend is not confined to one place, but is a global phenomenon. For example, in a study on job stress, burnout, and turnover motivation among urban workers in Canada, China, Malaysia, and Pakistan, the researcher found job stress and job-related stressors were notably related to turnover motivation in all locations (Jamal, 2010). Thus, the success of the organization is dependent upon the health and well-being of the workers. Stress and burnout must be addressed within the organization in order to ensure the long-term sustainability of the organization.

Summary

In this chapter, I reviewed how stress and burnout impact workers' physical health, and thus ability to work, as well as their workplace behaviors and job performance. Because of their wide-ranging effects, reducing stress and burnout is ultimately important to ensuring the success of the organization. It is therefore vital to implement measures to reduce stress and burnout within the organization, a topic I turn to in the remaining chapters. The first step in implementing such a plan, as I outline in the next chapter, is recognizing the wide-ranging signs and symptoms of stress and burnout, both among individuals and in organizational workforce trends as a whole.

CHAPTER 3

RECOGNIZING STRESS & BURNOUT

Now that we understand what stress and burnout are and how they impact the workplace, it is important to learn to recognize the signs and symptoms of stress and burnout, in order to be able to implement interventions appropriately. Indeed, the first step in any intervention or action plan to reduce stress and burnout should be to look for, identify, and note any signs and symptoms that arise both among individuals' health and job performance, and within organizational workforce trends more broadly.

Everyone is Different

The experience of burnout always changes because it depends on the influence burnout has on the individual worker's experience (Gustafsson, Norberg, & Strandberg, 2008). In other words, because everyone is different and comes with different experiences, frames of reference, and coping mechanisms, people will respond to situations differently, leading them to experience burnout differently.

Signs and Symptoms

Because individuals experience stress and burnout differently, there are a wide range of symptoms of stress and burnout. It is important to recognize these symptoms so that stress and burnout can be addressed. Recognizing symptoms requires paying attention to how people feel/what they experience, what they say, and how they act. Below, I list signs and symptoms to watch out for at the individual and organization levels.

Individually, workers may experience:

- Trouble sleeping, fatigue, and exhaustion, which can become extreme,

- Lack of energy,

- Annoyance, frustration, irritability, or anger/rage,

- Paranoia,

- Feeling numb or like you cannot connect with others,

- Feeling overwhelmed or like you cannot succeed,

- Decreased self-esteem and increased negative self-thoughts,

- Lack of self-confidence,

- Anxiety, depression, melancholy, or feelings of hopelessness, which may lead to suicide ideation,

- Emotional pain,

- Decreased passion, enjoyment, and enthusiasm in the work,

- Dissatisfaction in the work,

- Alcohol and substance use/abuse,

- Physical ailments/illness (e.g., headaches, colds, stomach problems, back aches, appetite changes, eyestrain, dizziness, restlessness, and trouble breathing),

- Lack of focus and/or concentration, or

- Memory problems.

In communication with others, workers may say:

- They are drained or physically tired,

- They are stressed out or frustrated,

- They feel tired/sick of the work they are doing,

- They are unsure what to do,

- They do not feel like they are making a difference,

- They are unwell/sick,

- They do not care about what they are doing or people they work with,

- They dread coming to work,

- They do not like their work or people they work with,

- They want to leave work, or

- They want to change roles/jobs.

In their actions, workers may:

- Appear distracted and unfocused,

- Be irritable, short-tempered, or hostile,

- Act indifferent, apathetic, or 'cold' toward others/their work,

- Socially withdraw from others,

- Appear stressed and overwhelmed,

- Appear anxious or "emotional,"

- Make inappropriate jokes about their work or joke about being stressed,

- Complain about their work or workload,

- Be slow or late to turn in work/get things done,

- Exhibit a decrease in work ethic,

- Fail to complete their work,

- Make mistakes in their work,

- Be late for work,

- Call in sick, or

- Request a transfer, early retirement, or quit their job.

Overtime, within the organization, these symptoms may manifest in:

- Decreased interpersonal relationships (among workers, between workers and management, and between workers and patients/clients),
- Increased interpersonal conflict,
- Low staff morale,
- Decreased productivity,
- Increased errors in work,
- Decreased quality/level of service to customers/clients/patients,
- Increased absences (calling in sick, being late),
- Decreased loyalty to the organization,
- Increased intent to relocate, intent to leave,
- Increased early retirement, or
- High turnover and attrition.

Coping Mechanisms/Strategies

Individuals' coping mechanism, the tools they use to deal with stress and burnout, are key to ensuring they succeed in the workplace. There are many coping mechanisms/strategies that can be employed to deal with stress and burnout. While I discuss specific strategies from the organizational perspective more in the next chapter, below I outline a few areas of focus that help to mitigate/reduce stress and burnout in the workplace, at the individual level:

- **Education:** Educating individuals at all levels of the organization on the signs and symptoms of stress and burnout will help them to self-identify when they are experiencing such symptoms or witness the symptoms in those around them. Individuals should take appropriate measures to seek support (both within and outside the institution) in order to combat workplace stress and burnout.

- **Interpersonal support:** Talking to and drawing support from others is an important strategy to tackle stress and burnout. Indeed, in one study that looked at a "collectivistic culture," where workers supported one another naturally due to their cultural backgrounds, workers experienced less stress and burnout (Jamal, 2010). Social interaction, such as being around friends, may also provide positive support that mitigates stress.

- **Work–life balance:** Focusing on developing and maintaining a healthy work–life balance is a preventative measure key to coping with stress and burnout effectively. Workers have to know how to give and take, and not just consistently give of themselves. Creating a balance evens out the stress that formulates into "work overload, understaff, over commitment and other imbalance that goes along with burnout" (Maslach, 2003, p. 240).

- **Hobbies/activities:** When individuals partake in activities that bring pleasure, it mitigates stress. This may occur inside or outside the workplace. Such activities could include music, reading, shopping, watching TV, sports, or other extracurricular activities.

- **Exercise/meditation:** Exercise, meditation, relaxation, and other similar activities have been shown to help reduce stress.

It is important to note that not all coping mechanisms are positive or healthy. Unhealthy or negative coping mechanisms include:

- Being combative,
- Cursing,
- Yelling,
- Withdrawing,
- Abusing substances/alcohol,
- Suicide,
- Irrational decisions, or
- Violence.

It is thus important to teach positive coping mechanisms to workers so that they do not resort to negative means to relieve stress and so that they can be successful in life (Laal & Aliramaie, 2010).

In another model, Jenaro, Flores, and Arias (2007) distinguished between problem-focused and emotional-focused coping methods. In problem-focused methods, individuals focus on the problem and find solutions to resolve the matter, a process that utilizes "planning, focusing on efforts to resolve situation, social support, personal growth and positive reinterpretation" (p. 82). In the latter, individuals use emotion to resolve the matter, often involving "religion, humor, alcohol-drug intake, disengagement, focus on and venting of emotions, acceptance, denial and restraint" (Jenaro et al., 2007, p. 82). In this model, we see that while some emotional-focused methods may be negative, there are still positive ways to harness emotion as coping mechanisms to reduce stress and burnout.

Ultimately, coping mechanisms are important for individuals to understand how to deal with stressful matters successfully in the workplace. There are alternative and religious strategies that individuals can utilize when in a hazardous environment (Laal & Aliramaie, 2010; Pieper & van Uden, 2012). Whether an employee decides to meditate, plan, or exercise, these methods address the main purpose, which is to relieve the high level of stress so they will become less burned out.

Summary

Recognizing the signs and symptoms of burnout are the first step in addressing the problem in any organization. It is both the responsibility of individuals and management to look for these symptoms, so they can be addressed early on. Early intervention is key to reducing stress and burnout. It is vital that organizations find ways to reduce stress in the workplace in order to decrease stress and therefore burnout among staff. Maintaining the well-being of the workforce is essential not only to ensure the well-being of staff, but also to ensure long-term organizational success and sustainability. In the next chapter, I look more practically at how organizations can create a healthy workplace to reduce stress and burnout.

CHAPTER 4

CREATING A HEALTHY WORKPLACE

It is important to acknowledge the impacts of stress and burnout in the workplace. As previously illustrated, there are a wide variety of ways that stress and burnout affect the workplace, as well as in how stress and burnout are expressed among workers. Because it is such an individual experience, stress and burnout can be brought on by a wide range of factors, and each worker is impacted differently by the responsibilities they hold and at different times during the work day and/or at home after they leave the workplace. In order to prevent stress and burnout, prevention (i.e., creating a healthy workplace) and early intervention are key. This requires both individuals and organizational leadership to consciously consider, monitor, and address stress and burnout on an ongoing basis within the workplace. In this chapter, I provide some practical ideas to address stress and burnout in the workplace.

Step 1: Identify Stress and Burnout

As discussed in Chapter 3, the first step in addressing stress and burnout is to educate individuals at all levels of the organization as well as leadership on the many signs and symptoms of burnout. Because stress and burnout can manifest in a wide variety of ways, as shown in Chapter 3, it is important that individuals as well as organizational leadership are vigilant and pay attention to behaviors in the workplace. Similarly, there are several job-related stressors that may prevent an individual from being successful, including "work overload, conflict of interest, inadequate resources, and unhealthy environment" (Jamal, 2010, p. 31).

With this in mind, organizations need to be more involved and aware of their employees' potential stress levels within the work arena. Workers and leadership must listen to each other and check in about how they are feeling in order to provide a means for communication about stress and burnout to occur. Stress is a serious condition, which can cause an individual to become physically or mentally ill. When an individual is not able to think clearly, they can make an irrational decision, which may affect their job and the company, and lead to feelings of dissatisfaction in the workplace (Jamal, 2010).

Apart from direct communication, there are also various organizational trends that can be used to indicate if staff are experiencing stress and burnout, including number of sick days and the rate of employee turnover. Organizations with high rates of sick days and employee turnover should consider how employees' mental and physical health is being impacted by the workplace, and whether stress and burnout are a factor in employees' health, job satisfaction, or decision to leave.

Often, when individuals are under large amounts of stress, they tend to become distant from others, cold, and possibly leave their job (Jamal, 2010; Potter et al., 2010). This can cause an organization to have a high turnover rate within the organization. Previous research indicates a high turnover rate likely results from employees being unhappy, lacking motivation, and feeling dissatisfied.

There are also various methods and tools available for assessing employee job satisfaction and wellbeing in the workplace. For example, Leiter and Maslach (2005) developed a method to help workers in human service occupations and other professionals address and decrease their burnout in the workplace. In this method, employees identify their problem areas in the workplace that are contributing to their stress and burnout using the My Relationship With Work test. In this test, employees develop a profile to assess their level of satisfaction and general wellbeing in relation to six areas: workload, control, reward, community, fairness, and values. The test consists of 10 questions that address each of the six areas of focus. The employee scores each individual area by selecting whether the question is a "match," "mismatch," or "just right," which are respectively coded 0, 1, or 2. Once the scores have been tallied up, the employee receives a score for each ranging from 0 to 20. These scores are then used for the employee to identify areas of their work life with which they are not in harmony, or which may be contributing to their feelings of stress and burnout in the workplace.

Step 2: Take Measures to Address Stress and Burnout

Once it is established staff are experiencing stress and burnout, it is important to implement interventions and measures to help staff recover, including providing adequate support. Such measures could include starting a training program, avoiding utilizing the same staff member, reducing the amount of hours worked, promoting teamwork, sharing experiences with others, providing time off, obtaining more volunteers, or encouraging involvement in various types of activity.

In Leiter and Maslach's (2005) method, they recommend that once the employees have identified their problem area(s) using the self-test they created, the employees and their managers should develop a plan of action to address the issue. This plan should consist of four main parts: defining the problem, setting objectives, taking action, and tracking progress (Leiter & Maslach, 2005). These four steps will get the employees on the path to recover from the situation and decrease burnout.

Step 3: Prevention is Key

However, the best way to manage stress and burnout is to prevent it by employing an organizational plan that promotes a healthy workplace and takes into account the impact of the organizational environment on workers' mental and physical health and wellbeing. There are ways to lighten the situation and keep employees happy (Jamal, 2010), and many different methods to help employees avoid accumulating stress which leads to burnout.

Increasing various activities in the workplace can help to combat stress and burnout. Oftentimes, private practice offices do not provide activities for employees, such as extracurricular activities, team-building days, or other activities that promote developing relationships and boosting staff morale. Research suggests that an active plan needs to be implemented to help enhance the working arena and keep employees' stress level low. Some of these activities include fitness training, occupational education, and encouragement among workers, which can help to prevent burnout (Hui et al., 2013).

The Role of Management

In every organization, the manager is the most important part of the company and regardless of their personal feelings, they need to be warm, caring, and understanding. Moreover, a manager's focal point should be the attributes that can enhance their workers' quality of work as a whole (Ejaz, Ejaz, Rehman, & Zaheer, 2009). It is a leader's duty to keep their employees influenced to stay motivated on a daily basis. In order for staff to satisfy their duties, they need to be equipped with the proper tools and leaders should always be encouraging to keep employees focused. Managers need to be well rounded and have background knowledge in their field in addition to their managerial style (Ejaz et al., 2009). There are many ways individuals can be motivated in their work performance (Lewicka & Wzkątek, 2010).

The research shows managers need to be efficient in their strategy to continue fulfilling the needs of their employees. According to one study, managers who have a high score as an effective leader are more knowledgeable of the scope of the company (Ejaz et al., 2009). Managers need to be involved with their employees and make sure they distribute different duties to staff to motivate them. A manager's success can determine their loyalty; however, they also need to be flexible in their schedule. Utilizing different rules and policies will encourage employees to work to their highest potential (Ejaz et al., 2009).

A key role of management is to make sure staff understand their roles and duties, to put forth clear expectations for work, and to set achievable goals in collaboration with staff. Zhang et al. (2013) suggested that job stressors such as role ambiguity and role conflict can cause an individual to decrease in working efficiently and possibly lead to resignation. Lack of clarity of job roles/tasks and overburdening workers with heavy workloads results in stress and burnout. Therefore, in order to help staff understand what are reasonable or unreasonable duties on a daily basis, management should have open discussion with staff about expectations and goals (Gustafsson et al., 2008). This will provide insight for both managers and staff as to what type of demands are achievable at work, thereby increasing efficiency and decreasing stress in the workplace.

Summary

In this chapter, I discussed practical ways that individuals and organizations can work to combat stress and burnout in the workplace. The first step is to make sure members of the organization at all levels are aware of and understand the signs and symptoms of burnout. Early intervention is key to reducing stress before burnout occurs. Organizations must provide interventions that decrease staff stress and burnout, or else they risk losing their employees because of ill health and/or job dissatisfaction.

Prevention can be achieved by putting measures in place to help relieve stress on an ongoing basis, such as increasing workplace activities, and by creating a healthy work environment that is supportive of staff and encourages healthy and positive behaviors. This cycles of prevention, monitoring, and intervention is ongoing and requires the organization to continually assess how workers are performing as well as the state of workers' physical and mental health. Ultimately, it is only with targeted prevention strategies and interventions for the management of stress and burnout that will ensure an organization is sustainable and successful in the long-term.

CHAPTER 5

BECOMING REJUVENATED AGAIN

There are so many reasons why burnout is a nation-wide concern. Many organizations are finding their employees are showing symptoms of or experiencing burnout. However, many organizations and individuals do not know exactly what to look for or how to decrease the chance of becoming burned out. Maslach (2003) and Freudenberger (1974), the initial experts who researched burnout, discovered that burnout can impact all industries of work and all job roles. However, those who work in the field of catering to people or human service tend to be impacted greater than those in other job roles or fields.

Dr. Darlynne Kerr

One of the main elements of burnout is prolonged stress resulting from the habitat of the work environment, lack of resources, and feeling overwhelmed with responsibilities from employers (Jamal, 2010). These different aspects, combined with the various personal situations that affect people in their everyday lives, can bring people to their breaking point. After conducting research, I was surprised to discover that many people do not realized that they have reached the point of being burned out. They just think they are stressed and tend to downplay the effects of that prolonged stress on their health and wellbeing and in their lives. The definition of burnout is having no sense of care, no sense of vitality, and no sense of self-confidence (Leiter & Maslach, 2005).

When people experience stress that is drawn out over a long time period, they start to display different signs that fall under the main three categories of burnout: emotional exhaustion, depersonalization, and personal accomplishment (Maslach & Jackson, 1981, p. 100). These attributes manifest in different signs and symptoms, which people start to display when they are becoming burned out, including: calling in sick to work frequently, constantly coming in late, not preforming at 100%, expressing negative thoughts or ideas, being isolated, and failing to show concern for self and others. Indeed, organizations and individuals sometimes do not fully understand the effects that burnout can have on a person. Burnout can cause a person to become physically ill, mentally ill, and have different body aches and pains—all due to prolonged stress.

One of the key elements to healing from burnout is to understand how it can be decreased. This is important so that both organizations and individuals may experience a better work environment, and so individuals can monitor themselves and begin to reduce the prolonged stress in their lives. There are many ways that an individual or organization can decrease stress, however not all ways lead to sustained healing. Indeed, some methods of alleviating stress may cause negative outcomes over time and lead to other health problems, complications, or issues. The most effective approach is to try to adopt positive methods to obtain positive outcomes (Laal & Aliramaie, 2010; Maslach, 2003). Some positive actions individuals may engage in to reduce stress include:

- Reading,
- Exercising,
- Dancing,
- Praying,
- Meditating,
- Writing,
- Talking with others, or
- Doing an activity you love.

Negative behaviors that may lead to negative outcomes include:

- Substance use,
- Smoking,
- Drinking alcohol,

- Yelling and fighting, or

- Throwing things (Laal & Aliramaie, 2010; Maslach, 2003).

At the organizational level, positive actions may include:

- Setting up time for games and team-building activities,

- Having team nights/holiday parties,

- Having office gatherings,

- Hosting activities where employees can bring their families,

- Incentives/trips,

- Building a relationship with employees– getting to know them genuinely),

- Including employees in the decision-making process,

- Providing positive feedback– constructive, with a plan how to accomplish shared goals, or

- Conducting encouragement workshops (Barber, 2010; Klupas, 2009).

Conversely, negative organizational actions (or lack of action) include:

- Not setting up activities for employees (games, events, etc.),
- Not providing incentives or rewards for employees,
- Not listening to employees,
- Providing negative feedback or no feedback,
- Not providing direction or clear action plans,
- Delegating responsibility but no assistance with direction, or
- Not including employees in the decision-making process (Barber, 2010; Klupsas, 2009).

The encouraging aspect of this issue is that there are ways that people and organizations can create positive outcomes for themselves. For businesses to be successful, they must learn how to help their employees and decrease the chances of employees getting burned out. Utilizing this information will help organizations and individuals rejuvenate themselves, by decreasing the level of burnout being experienced and helping individuals to take control of their lives and better cope with stress.

It is important individuals do not become overwhelmed with what is happening in their lives—this is key to reducing and eliminating burnout. By knowing the signs and symptoms of burnout, as well as how to decrease stress proactively, organizations will be well on the path to ensuring they have a vibrant and healthy workforce. Similarly, individuals will be able to stop and ask for help and take the appropriate measures before the stress gets too much, reducing the risk of burnout.

CLOSING REMARKS

Employees in major organizations and private practices face a myriad of challenges with stress and burnout. There have been countless situations where employees have suffered from the different attributes of burnout, and many have committed suicide due to the pressures of the workplace environment both within the United States and abroad. Both part- and full-time workers in most sectors in the Unites States continue to report high levels of job stress, and figures continue to rise. Burnout is very costly both to the individual and the organization, affecting workers' health, job performance, employee satisfaction and retention, and ultimately, organizational success.

This book has provided an evidence-based guide for individuals and organizations so they may learn to recognize, address, and manage stress and burnout in the workplace. Key to doing so is understanding what stress and burnout are, as well as the wide range of signs and symptoms that may indicate a worker is experiencing stress and/or burnout. Ultimately, individuals and organizations must work together on a continual basis to monitor workers' wellbeing and to implement strategies and interventions for the prevention and management of stress and wellbeing.

Eight Key Themes

In this section, I provide a brief recap of eight key points concerning stress and burnout for individuals and organizations presented in this book.

1. Effects

Stress and burnout have significant, long-lasting negative effects for both individuals and organizations. These effects range from poor health to job dissatisfaction, to reduced performance/efficiency, to high employee turnover and decreased organizational success. These effects are costly for the organization and impede organizational sustainability.

2. Causes

There are many causes of stress and burnout. A number of factors influence individuals' stress levels which, when high over the long-term, may lead to burnout, such as the workplace environment, relationships and interactions with others in the workplace, the nature of the job itself, role ambiguity/conflict, workload, and compensation/benefits.

3. Symptoms

Stress and burnout are expressed in different ways. There are many different signs and symptoms for burnout, ranging from fatigue, short-temperedness/irritability, and depression/anxiety, to decreased productivity, job performance, motivation, and satisfaction in the workplace, to absenteeism and employee turnover. It is important to learn to recognize the signs and symptoms of stress to be able to intervene early on and prevent burnout from occurring.

4. Affects Everyone

Stress and burnout can occur in any role, level, or kind of organization. Stress and burnout are not exclusive to any one job role, level, organizational type, or sector. Stress and burnout are a global phenomenon that impacts many different kinds of workers in different fields. However, individuals working in service roles such as health care may experience higher levels of stress and burnout. Any individual can experience stress or burnout, regardless of their level of training/education, level of experience, preexisting mental/physical health issues, personal characteristics, or background. Both part-time and full-time employees may experience stress and burnout.

5. Joint Responsibility

Both individuals and organizations are responsible for addressing stress and burnout. Preventing and managing stress and burnout require a collaborative effort between individual workers and organizational leadership. Individuals must be cognizant of their own health and wellbeing and take steps to address the situation if they become stressed in the workplace. Organizations must provide a healthy workplace and provide support for all workers to manage stress and burnout. Leadership is especially important in effecting organizational change and interventions that promote a healthy workplace and address stress and burnout. All levels of the organization must work together and communicate effectively with each other.

6. Planning

Managing stress and burnout requires a plan. Individuals and organizations should work together to create a plan to address stress and burnout in the workplace on an ongoing basis. This plan should include means to assess levels of stress, identify factors impacting stress, set healthy objectives/goals, take action, and track progress. Such a plan should be cyclical and ongoing, and not a one-off endeavor. Without a targeted plan, individuals and organizations will not have a coherent means to address the situation, and will continue to be impacted negatively both at the individual and organizational level by the outcomes related to stress and burnout.

7. Prevention

Prevention is key. The old saying "prevention is the best medicine" is true in the case of stress and burnout. Providing a healthy workplace and consistently monitor self/others' stress levels is key in avoiding burnout. It is much easier and more effective to decrease workers' stress levels early on than to try to cope with burnout after the fact. Indeed, it is the cumulative effects of stress over the long-term that lead to burnout. Avoiding burnout means eliminating costs to the individual and the workplace, and improving worker satisfaction, wellbeing, productivity, performance, and retention.

8. Rejuvenation

It is possible, if deliberate steps are taken, to recover from stress and burnout to feel rejuvenated once again. There are many things that individuals and organisations can do to help heal from stress and burnout. It is important that the actions taken promote positive behaviors that heal burnout and replenish energy sustainably, rather than negative behaviors that may provide temporary relief but, in the long run, exacerbate the problem or lead to other forms of illness.

Tips and Recommendations

In this evidence-based book, I explored the various facets of stress and burnout in the workplace. This exploration provides a greater understanding of the phenomenon, and aims to provide insight for employees and management on the contributing factors that impact stress and burnout to assist them with this alarming issue. Here I provide a brief list of tips for individuals and organizations to help decrease stress and burnout within their organizations. These activities can be undertaken daily, weekly, or monthly and should be reviewed on an ongoing basis. It is important to note that these tips are not exhaustive. Rather, they offer ideas of where to start when it comes to reducing stress and burnout.

Ideally, individuals and organizations should assess the particular risk of burnout for their specific contexts, looking at the stressors, triggers, and specific risks in their work environment and lives. By doing this, a plan can be made to address how to prevent, cope with or manage, and reduce burnout. Individuals should think about what specific things work best for them to reduce stress, and develop their own toolkits of resources/activities as their "go-to" in times of stress. These tips are followed by a list of recommendations for future scholarship to expand our knowledge of stress and burnout in the future.

Tips for Individuals

The following list provides tips for individuals to reduce stress and therefore burnout in their lives through positive activities. It is important for individuals to try out different things until they figure out what works for them.

- Take short, effective periodic breaks,
- Exercise several days out of the week,

- Read during your free time,

- Listen to jokes– laughter is the best medicine!

- Listen to music that is inspiring,

- Take a 5-10 minute walk,

- Have a picture or write down what you are striving for and look at it as a reminder,

- Make time in your daily schedule to manage your stress level,

- Write out your goals and what you want to accomplish,

- Outdoor activities,

- Extra-curricular activities,

- Entertain those things that are fulfilling and keeps you busy,

- Talk to a mentor or someone you trust for advice, or

- Pray, meditate, and rest.

Tips for Organizations

The following tips can be implemented by managers of organizations to help reduce stress and burnout in their organizations:

- Provide non-work-related downtime for all staff,
- Have optional team nights,
- Have daily or weekly breakdowns of staff day,
- Include staff in decisions/ask for their opinions,
- Give staff members time off to recuperate,
- Monitor employees throughout the day,
- Have areas or break rooms that allow different activities to relieve stress,
- Try different methods to assist in relieving stress,
- Host potluck meals or other team-building activities,
- Provide incentives and rewards to staff, or
- Monitor staff by utilizing the Maslach Burnout Inventory (MBI) assessment.

Recommendations for Scholarship

More research is needed to fully understand stress and burnout within the workplace. Based on the existing literature as well as my own doctoral research, ideas for future research include:

- Research examining administrative positions;
- Research specifically assessing male, female, or minority populations;
- Comparative studies between geographical regions;
- Research comparing micromanaged versus non-micromanaged work environments;
- Research examining administrative employees/management's work performance and motivation level within direct marketing occupations;
- Longitudinal research examining the efficacy of stress/burnout interventions over time.

Final Thoughts

In our contemporary world, we do not have to look far to find a source of stress. It is no surprise, then, that stress and burnout continue to be such pressing issues in the workplace. Job stress, the source of burnout, can manifest in many ways, leading to various physical, behavioral, and emotional ailments. Stress and burnout can impact employees' work behaviors, leading to a decline in employees' work performance and satisfaction. This, in turn, has high costs for the organization, including long-term outcomes such as organizational success. It is imperative that both individuals and organizations consider how stress and burnout are affecting them, and take measures to reduce stress and burnout in the workplace. It is my hope that this book has provided a tool for individuals and organizations to embark upon this endeavor, and a starting point to ultimately increase the health and wellbeing of workers everywhere.

RECOMMENDED RESOURCES

There are a number of organizations and resources that provide assistance for individuals coping with stress and burnout. Counseling and other types of therapeutic care may be provided by various organizations and health providers both inside and outside the workplace. There are also a number of resources that can be found by searching the Internet using phrases such as "how to cope with stress and burnout" or "stress and burnout in the workplace." Below are some suggestions for individuals to help them get started. If you feel you are experiencing stress or burnout, know you are not alone. Contact your employer, GP, or other health professional so you can get the help you need.

Organizations (South Carolina):

Bridge of Hope

418-A Barr Road

Lexington, SC 29072

Faith Presbyterian Church Counseling Center

1500 Lady Street

Columbia, SC 29201

Websites:

15 Minutes 4 Me- Daily self-help program

https://www.15minutes4me.com

The Clinical Advisor- List of online tools and mobile apps to reduce burnout and stress

https://www.clinicaladvisor.com/home/topics/practice-management-information-center/7-online-tools-and-mobile-apps-recommended-to-reduce-burnout-stress/

Stress and Burnout Self-Tests:

MindTools

https://www.mindtools.com/pages/article/newTCS_08.htm

15 Minutes 4 Me

https://www.15minutes4me.com/stress-free/burn-out-test-if-youre-stressed-out-burnout-exhausted-or-burnt-out/

Psychology Today

https://www.psychologytoday.com/us/tests/career/burnout-test-service-fields

Maslach Burnout Inventory

https://www.mindgarden.com/117-maslach-burnout-inventory

Educational Resources:

Banishing Burnout: Six Strategies for Improving Your Relationship With Work by Michael Leiter and Christina Maslach
https://www.amazon.com/Banishing-Burnout-Strategies-Improving-Relationship /dp/0470448776

Burnout: The Cost of Caring by Christina Maslach
https://www.amazon.com/Burnout-Cost-Caring-Christina-Maslach/dp/1883536359

Burnout: The Secret to Unlocking the Stress Cycle by Amelia Nagoski and Emily Nagoski
https://www.amazon.com/dp/B07DT4GW16/ref=dp-kindle-redirect?_encoding=UTF 8&btkr=1

"Caregiver Stress and Burnout: Tips for Regaining Your Energy, Optimism, and Hope" by HelpGuide.org
https://www.helpguide.org/articles/stress/caregiver-stress-and-burnout.htm/

"How to Deal with Stress and Burnout in Your Job Search" by Rachel Montanez

https://www.forbes.com/sites/rachelmontanez/2019/01/30/how-to-deal-with-stress-and-burnout-in-your-job-search/#386994ed7f21

REFERENCES

Barber, T. (2010). Inspire your employees now. *Business Week Online, 10.*

Ejaz, S. K., Ejaz, S. A., Rehman, K. U., & Zaheer, A. (2009). Evaluating effective leadership qualities of managers in day-to-day work of banking sector in Pakistan. *International Journal of Management and Marketing Research, 2*(1), 103–111.

Ekstedt, M., & Fagerberg, I. (2005). Lived experiences of the time preceding burnout. *Journal of Advanced Nursing, 49*(1), 59–67.

Engelbrecht, S. (2005). *Motivation and burnout in human service work: The case of midwifery in Denmark* (Unpublished doctoral dissertation). Roskilde University.

Freudenberger, H. J. (1974). Staff burn-out. *Journal of Social Issues, 50*(1), 159–165.

Freudenberger, H. J. (1975). The staff burnout syndrome in alternative institutions. *Psychotherapy Theory, 12,* 72–73.

Galanakis, M., Moraitou, M., Garivalkis, F. J., & Stalikas, A. (2009). Factorial structure and psychometric properties of the Maslach Burnout Inventory (MBI) in Greek midwives. *Europe's Journal of Psychology, 4,* 52–70.

Green, A. E., Miller, E. A., & Aarons, G. A. (2013). Transformational leadership moderates the relationship between emotional exhaustion and turnover intention among community mental health providers. *Community Mental Health Journal, 49*(4), 373–379.

Gustafsson, G., Norberg, A., & Strandberg, G. (2008). Meanings of becoming and being burnout: Phenomenological-hermeneutic interpretation of female healthcare personnel's narratives. *Scandinavian Journal of Caring Sciences, 22*(4), 520–528.

Hazell, K. W. (2010). *Job stress, burnout, job satisfaction, and intention to leave among registered nurses employed in hospital settings in the state of Florida* (Doctoral dissertation). Available from ProQuest Dissertations and Theses database (UMI No. 3406218)

Hui, W., Li, L., Yang, W., Fei, G., Xue, Z., & Lie, W. (2013). Factors associated with burnout among Chinese hospital doctors: A cross-sectional study. *BMC Public Health, 13*(1), 1–8. doi:10.1186/1471-2458-13-786

Jamal, M. (2010). Burnout among Canadian, Chinese, Malaysian and Pakistani employees: An empirical examination. *International Management Review, 6*(1), 31–41.

Jayson, S. (2012). Burnout up among employees. Retrieved from http://www.usatoday.com/story/news/nation/2012/10/23/stress-burnout-employees/1651897

Jenaro, C., Flores, N., & Arias, B. (2007). Burnout and coping in human service practitioners. *Professional Psychology Research and Practice, 36*(1), 80–87.

Kerr, D. (2017). *An exploratory study of administrative staff's experiences with burnout in private practice in the Southeast region* (Unpublished doctoral dissertation). Argosy University, Atlanta, GA.

Klupsas, F. (2009). Production employees' motivation: Strengthening news under changing conditions. *Management Theory & Studies for Rural Business & Infrastructure Development, 19*(4), 36–44.

Laal, M., & Aliramaie, N. (2010). Nursing and coping with stress. *International Journal of Collaborative Research on Internal Medicine & Public Health, 2*(5), 168–181.

Lambert, E. G., Hogan, N. L., Cheeseman, K., & Barton-Bellessa, S. M. (2013). The relationship between job stressors and job involvement among correctional staff: A test of the job strain model. *The Howard Journal of Criminal Justice, 52*(1), 19–38.

Lee, R., Lovell, B., & Brotheridge, C. M. (2010). Tenderness and steadiness: Relating job and interpersonal demands and resources with burnout and physical symptoms of stress in Canadian physicians. *Journal of Applied Social Psychology, 40*(9), 2319–2342.

Leiter, M. P., & Maslach, C. (2005). A mediation model of job burnout. *Research Companion to Organizational Health Psychology,* 544.

Lewicka, D., & Wzkątek, S. A. (2010). Motivating employee versus challenges of contemporary economy. *Tiltai/Bridges, 50*(1), 39–41.

Maslach, C. (2003). *Burnout: The cost of caring.* Englewood Cliffs, NJ: Spectrum.

Maslach, C., & Jackson, S. (1981). The measurement of experienced burnout. *Journal of Organizational Behavior, 2*(2), 99–113.

Maslach, C., & Leiter, M. P. (2005). *Banishing burnout: Six strategies for improving your relationship with work.* San Francisco, CA: Wiley.

Maslach, C., & Pines, A. (1978). Characteristics of staff burnout in mental health setting. *American Psychiatric Association, 29*(4), 233–237.

Maslach, C., Schaufeli, W. B., & Leiter, M. P. (2001). Job burnout. *Annual Review of Psychology, 52*, 397–422.

Michie, S. (2002). Causes and management of stress at work. *Occupational and Environmental Medicine, 59*(1), 67–72.

Nixon, A. E., Mazzola, J. J., Bauer, J., Krueger, J. R., & Spector, P. E. (2011). Can work make you sick? A meta-analysis of the relationships between job stressors and physical symptoms. *Work & Stress, 25*(1), 1–22. doi:10.10 80/02678373.2011.569175

Pieper, J. Z., & van Uden, M. H. (2012). "Whenever God shines his light on me...": Religious coping in clinical healthcare institutions. *Mental Health, Religion & Culture, 15*(4), 403–416.

Pines, A. M. (1993). Burnout: An existential perspective. In W. B. Schaufeli, C. Maslach, & T. Marek (Eds.), *Professional burnout: Recent developments in theory and research* (pp. 35–51). Washington, DC: Taylor & Francis.

Potter, P., Deshields, T., Divanbeigi, J., Berger, J., Cipriano, D., Norris, L., & Olsen, S. (2010). Compassion fatigue and burnout: Prevalence among oncology nurses. *Clinical Journal of Oncology Nursing, 14*(5), 56–62.

Sohail, M., & Rehman, C. A. (2015). Stress and health at the workplace: A review of the literature. *Journal of Business Studies Quarterly, 6*(3), 94–121.

Venturi, R. (2014). Burnout in France: Focus turned to workplace health after spate of suicides. *Guardian Professional.*

Weaver, J. (2003). Job stress, burnout on the rise layoffs, long hours taking their toll on workers. *NBC News.* Retrieved from http://www.nbcnews.com/id/3072410/ns/business-us_business/t/job-stress-burnout-rise/#.U7X2Y2ivKfR

Zhang, R., Tsingan, L., & Zhang, L. (2013). Role stressors and job attitudes: A mediated model of leader-member exchange. *Journal of Social Psychology, 153*(5), 560–576. doi:10.1080/00224545.2013.778812

AUTHOR BIOGRAPHY

Dr. Darlynne Kerr has worked in the healthcare arena for over 15 years. Working in healthcare provides Darlynne with a level of satisfaction as she can help others achieve their goals in life. As a teenager, she worked at Planned Parenthood, and was inspired by the impact she had on the lives of young women experiencing hardship. That experience served as the driving force to pursue a career in health, so she could help individuals overcome the challenges they face to progress to a higher level in life. Since that time, she has held various roles in different avenues within the healthcare sector, including customer service, entertainment, hospitality, management, marketing, teaching, and insurance, and has recently ventured into being an entrepreneur. As a marketing manager, Darlynne represents Fortune 100 companies. This aspect of her career has taught her a lot. Here, she develops, trains, and coaches people daily, giving her insight into the psychology behind human behavior, in addition to helping individuals to find solutions to enhance their lives.

Darlynne's journey in education began in New York, her home state. She received a Bachelor of Arts Degree in Comparative Humanities in 2003 from SUNY Old Westbury. She then left New York and ventured down south, ending up in Atlanta, GA, where she attended Argosy University and finished her Master's in Business Management in 2010. Business management has always been a part of her focus, as she has always said that if she runs her own business, she needs to know the ins and outs. While studying for management marketing, Darlynne became very interesting in the processes of how to present ideas and thoughts to the community. She continued her education with Argosy University to earn her Doctorate in Business Administration in 2017. Darlynne's doctoral dissertation was published in 2019 by ProQuest.

Printed in the United States
by Baker & Taylor Publisher Services